MAPPING THE EARTH

MAPPING EARTH'S CONTINENTS

BY DWAYNE HICKS

Gareth Stevens
PUBLISHING

Please visit our website, www.garethstevens.com. For a free color catalog of all our high-quality books, call toll free 1-800-542-2595 or fax 1-877-542-2596.

Library of Congress Cataloging-in-Publication Data

Names: Hicks, Dwayne, cartographer.
Title: Mapping earth's continents / Dwayne Hicks.
Description: New York : Gareth Stevens, 2023. | Series: Mapping the earth | Includes index.
Identifiers: LCCN 2021037778 (print) | LCCN 2021037779 (ebook) | ISBN 9781538278093 (library binding) | ISBN 9781538278079 (paperback) | ISBN 9781538278086 (6 pack) | ISBN 9781538278109 (ebook)
Subjects: LCSH: Continents–Maps. | LCGFT: World atlases.
Classification: LCC G1046.C1 H5 2023 (print) | LCC G1046.C1 (ebook) | DDC 912–dc23/eng/20211021
LC record available at https://lccn.loc.gov/2021037778
LC ebook record available at https://lccn.loc.gov/2021037779

Published in 2023 by
Gareth Stevens Publishing
29 E. 21st Street
New York, NY 10010

Portions of this work were originally authored by Todd Bluthenthal and published as *Earth's Continents.* All new material in this edition authored by Dwayne Hicks.

Designer: Tanya Dellaccio
Editor: Kristen Nelson

Photo credits: Cover Peter Hermes Furian/Shutterstock.com; pp. 2–24 (background texture) Triff/Shutterstock.com; pp. 5, 7, 9, 11, 13, 15, 17, 19 (map) Maxger/Shutterstock.com; p. 7 Yuriy Chertok/Shutterstock.com; p. 9 astudio/Shutterstock.com; p. 11 nikitsin.smugmug.com/Shutterstock.com; p. 13 SL-Photography/Shutterstock.com; p. 15 StefanRenner/Shutterstock.com; p. 17 Vladimir Payusov/Shutterstock.com; p. 19 Claudio Soldi/Shutterstock.com; p. 21 Sean Pavone/Shutterstock.com.

Printed in the United States of America

CPSIA compliance information: Batch #CSGS23: For further information contact Gareth Stevens, New York, New York at 1-800-542-2595.

CONTENTS

Boldface words appear in the glossary.

Seven Landmasses

Continents are very large landmasses. Earth has seven continents. Each continent is a large piece of land and the islands that **surround** it. The continents cover about one-third of the planet. Water covers the rest of Earth.

ARCTIC OCEAN
NORTH AMERICA
EUROPE
ASIA
ATLANTIC OCEAN
AFRICA
PACIFIC OCEAN
SOUTH AMERICA
INDIAN OCEAN
AUSTRALIA
SOUTHERN OCEAN
ANTARCTICA

Highs and Lows

Asia makes up about one-third of Earth's land and is the largest continent. Asia is home to Mount Everest. It's the highest mountain on Earth! The Dead Sea is also in Asia. Its shore is the lowest land on the planet.

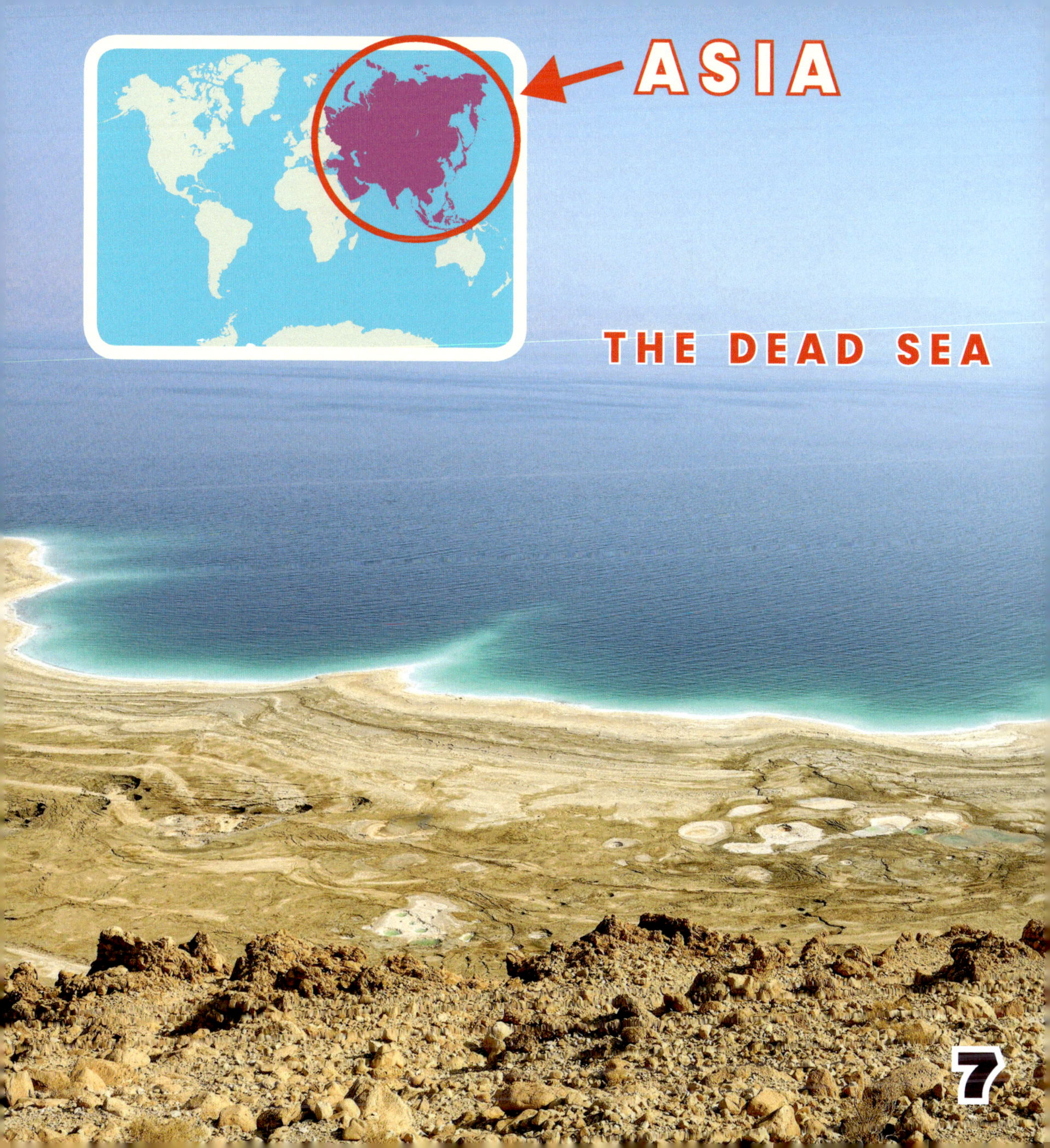
ASIA
THE DEAD SEA

Rivers and Deserts

Africa is the second-largest continent. It has two of the longest rivers in the world—the Nile and the Congo. Africa is also home to the Sahara Desert. It is the largest hot desert in the world. Africa's island of Madagascar is one of the largest islands in the world.

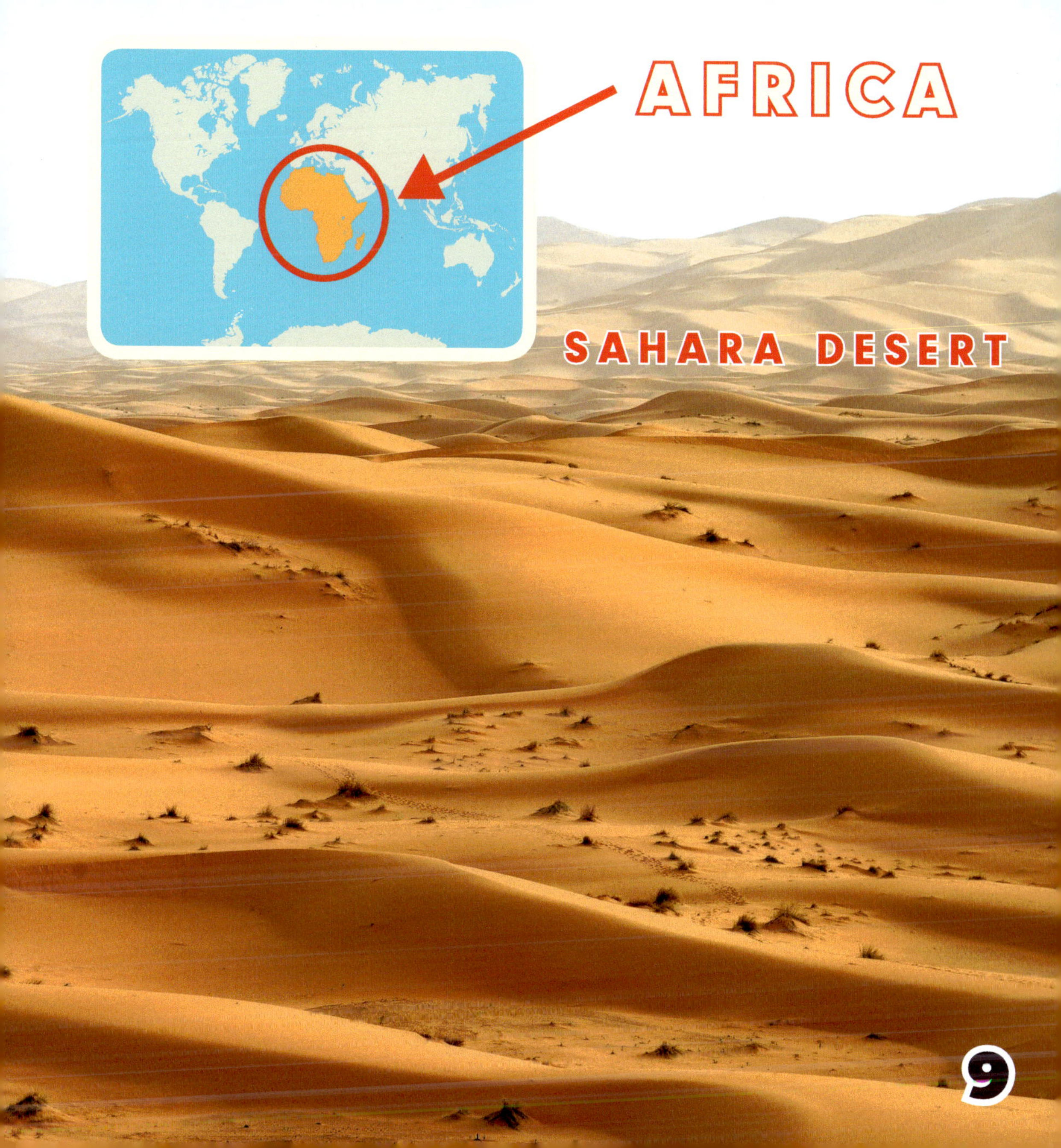
AFRICA
SAHARA DESERT

Big Lakes, Big Gulf

North America is the third-largest continent. It has the largest **freshwater** lakes in the world. They are called the Great Lakes. The **Gulf** of Mexico is also part of North America. It's the biggest gulf in the world. Many people live near these bodies of water.

NORTH AMERICA

LAKE SUPERIOR— THE LARGEST GREAT LAKE

The Amazon Rain Forest

South America is the fourth-largest continent. The Amazon River in South America is the longest river in the world. The Amazon River is surrounded by **rain forest**. The Amazon Rain Forest is the biggest rain forest in the world. It's home to many kinds of creatures.

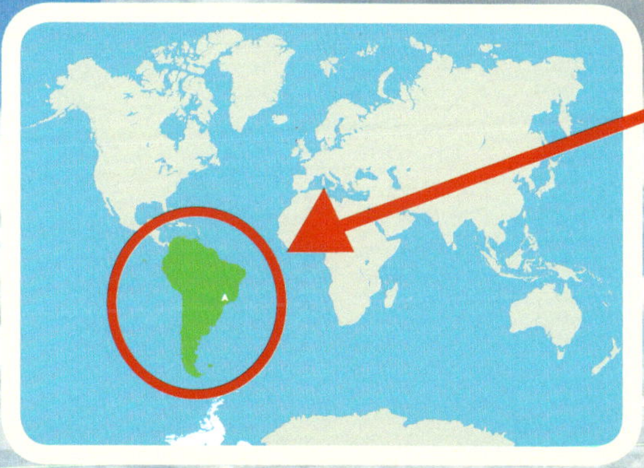

SOUTH AMERICA

AMAZON RAIN FOREST

An Icy Desert

Antarctica is the fifth-largest continent. It is the coldest, driest continent. It's surrounded by the Southern Ocean. It's almost completely covered by icy desert. The South Pole is in Antarctica. Not many people live in Antarctica. Scientists work there. Penguins live there!

ANTARCTICA

SOUTH POLE

Mountain Ranges

Europe is the sixth-largest continent. It is **separated** from Asia by the Ural Mountains. This mountain **range** runs through the country of Russia. Russia is so big that it's part of both continents! Europe is also home to a mountain range called the Alps.

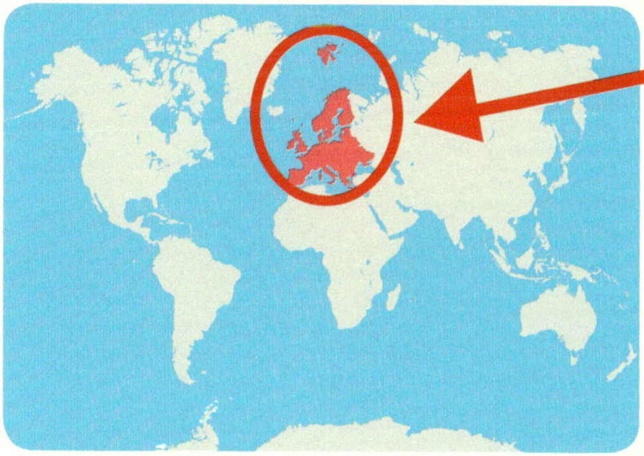
EUROPE

URAL
MOUNTAINS

Reefs and Rocks

Australia might be the smallest continent, but it is home to the largest coral reef in the world. The Great Barrier Reef is made up of many smaller reefs. Uluru is also in Australia. It's a huge landform far out in the desert. Many people visit it every year.

AUSTRALIA

ULURU

People Around the World

More than 4.5 **billion** people live in Asia. That's more than half of the people in the world! Nearly 580 **million** people live in North America. Antarctica is home to only about 1,000 people at a time! Most are scientists.

TOKYO, JAPAN, ASIA

GLOSSARY

billion: a thousand millions, or 1,000,000,000

freshwater: water that is not salty

gulf: a part of an ocean or sea that reaches into the land

million: a thousand thousands, or 1,000,000

rain forest: a forest that gets large amounts of rain every year

range: a line of mountains

separate: to be made into parts

surround: to be around on all or most sides

FOR MORE INFORMATION

BOOKS

Hernando, Mario Cuesta. *Antarctica: A Continent of Wonder.* Westminster, MD: Prestel Publishing, 2021.

National Kids. *My First Atlas of the World.* Washington, D.C.: National Geographic Kids, 2018.

Vallepur, Shalini. *North America.* New York, NY: Enslow Publishing, 2021.

WEBSITES

DK Findout! Continents
www.dkfindout.com/us/earth/continents/
Learn much more about the continents on this informative site, which includes interactive maps of the continents.

Ducksters: Geography
www.ducksters.com/geography/
This site provides a wealth of information about the continents.

Publisher's note to educators and parents: Our editors have carefully reviewed these websites to ensure that they are suitable for students. Many websites change frequently, however, and we cannot guarantee that a site's future contents will continue to meet our high standards of quality and educational value. Be advised that students should be closely supervised whenever they access the Internet.

INDEX